Vulture View

April Pulley Sayre ✦ *illustrated by* Steve Jenkins

Henry Holt and Company
NEW YORK

The sun is rising.

Up, up.

It heats the air.

Up, up.

Wings stretch wide
to catch a ride
on warming air.
Going where?

Up, up!

Turkey vultures tilt, soar, scan
to find the food that vultures can . . .

. . . eat!

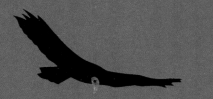

That snake over there?

No, no.

That fox over there?

No, no.

That bear over there?
No, no.

Vultures smell the air.
They sniff, search, seek
for foods that . . .

. . . REEK!

Those fragrant flowers?

No, no.

That spicy smoke?
No, no.

That stinky dead deer?
Yes, yes!

Vultures like a mess.

They land and dine.

Rotten is fine.

They eat, then clean.

Splash! Dry. Preen.

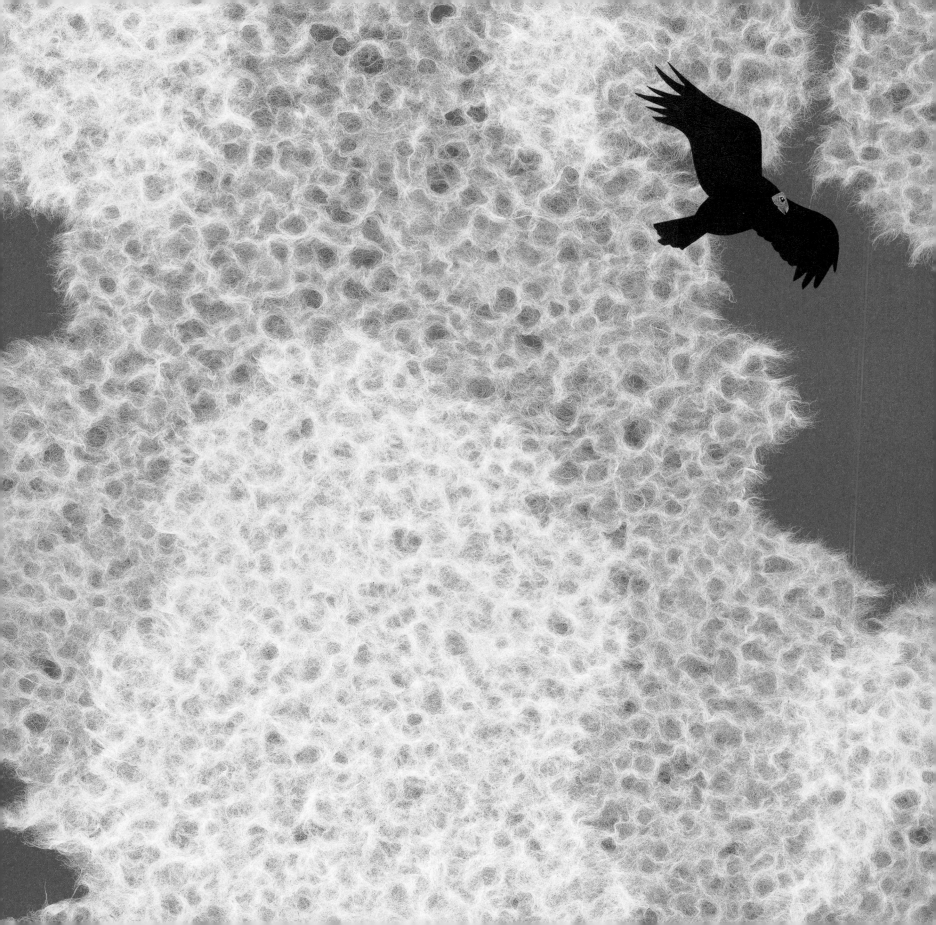

They hop, flap, soar
to look for more.
All afternoon.
But soon . . .

. . . the sun starts to sink.

Down, down.

The air starts to cool.

Down, down.

Wings glide, wings ride

through cooling air.

Going where?

Going **down**, down, down!

The vultures gather in vulture trees,
settle and sleep, like families.

Until . . .

. . . the morning sun rises.

Up, up.

It heats the air.

Up, up.

Wings stretch wide

to catch a ride

on warming air.

Going where?

Up, up!

Get to Know Vultures

Soaring Up, Up, Up!

Turkey vultures, which hold their wings in a distinctive V-shape, are among the most graceful soaring birds on earth. When the sun heats air near the ground, this warmed air rises in pockets, called thermals. Vultures hop, leap, flap, then stretch out their wings like sails, allowing the rising air to help lift them as they spiral upward.

Then they soar. Thermals form over fields, grasslands, cities, and even parking lots. As thermals rise, they can slide up hillsides. So you may see vultures rising along hillsides, lofted by warm air. Turkey vultures also get lift by taking advantage of wind that blows toward the hillside, then is deflected upward by the sloped ground.

As the sun sets, air cools and sinks. Breezes break up thermals and make it difficult for the vultures to maintain altitude. They settle in for the night. They sleep together in groups of ten or more.

The Vulture Family

Turkey vultures (scientific name *Cathartes aura*) belong to the family *Cathartidae*, which has seven species, including the black vulture and California condor. Adult turkey vultures have red faces, while immature ones have gray faces. Vultures in general have very few feathers on their faces, heads, or necks. Scientists believe this has to do with what they eat. When a vulture pokes its head neck-deep into a carcass, it can get messy. Feathers would be hard to clean.

Nature's Cleanup Crew

Unlike hawks and owls, turkey vultures have weak claws that are not suited for killing animals. Turkey vultures are scavengers. They eat carrion—dead animals that have been killed by accidents, diseases, or predators. As vultures eat, they break apart carcasses into smaller pieces. These smaller pieces can be more easily scavenged by mice, beetles, fly larvae, and worms. The rest of the carcass is decomposed by single-celled organisms and ultimately becomes part of the soil.

Turkey vultures find food by sight and smell. They can safely eat rotten food that would make a human sick. Scientists aren't sure how, but the vulture's body sterilizes the food, killing off dangerous organisms.

Although vultures are attracted to messy food, the birds themselves are very clean. They bathe and preen regularly to keep themselves tidy.

Family Life and Range

Turkey vultures nest in caves, cliffs, hollow trees, and abandoned buildings. They usually lay one to three eggs. Both the male and female take turns keeping the eggs warm and, later, feeding the young. Nine or so weeks after hatching, the young leave the nest to test their skills in the air.

In summer these birds range from southern Canada through most of the continental United States. Many of them migrate to South America for the winter. Unlike California condors, which are endangered, turkey vultures are increasing in number and are expanding their range northward, perhaps as a result of global climate change.

Heads-Up, Young Scientists!

Not much is known about the biology of turkey vultures. There isn't a great deal of information about how they communicate with one another, or what their lives are like during winter. All this, and more, needs scientific study.

To learn more, you can begin by checking the Turkey Vulture Society's Web site: www.vulturesociety.homestead.com.

You can also celebrate Turkey Vultures at these five festivals:
Branson Vulture Venture in Missouri (February);
Hinckley Buzzard Festival in Ohio (March);
Kern River Valley Turkey Vulture Festival in California (September or October);
Makanda Vulture Festival in Illinois (October);
Wenonah Buzzard Festival in New Jersey (March).

For all the underappreciated cleaner uppers in the world;
and for Chris and Becky, who were "vulched" with us in Texas.

—A. P. S.

For Jamie

—S. J.

MY THANKS TO THE FOLLOWING REVIEWERS:
Lloyd Kiff, Science Director of the Peregrine Fund; Dr. Keith L. Bildstein, Director of Conservation Science at the Acopian Center for Conservation Learning at Hawk Mountain Sanctuary; Dr. Jim Fraser, Professor of Wildlife Science at Virginia Tech; and Gerald W. Winegrad, Vice President for Policy at the American Bird Conservancy.

Henry Holt and Company, LLC, *Publishers since 1866*
175 Fifth Avenue, New York, New York 10010
www.HenryHoltKids.com

Henry Holt® is a registered trademark of Henry Holt and Company, LLC.
Text copyright © 2007 by April Pulley Sayre
Illustrations copyright © 2007 by Steve Jenkins
All rights reserved. Distributed in Canada by H. B. Fenn and Company Ltd.

Library of Congress Cataloging-in-Publication Data
Sayre, April Pulley.
Vulture view / April Pulley Sayre ; illustrated by Steve Jenkins.—1st ed.
p.   cm.
ISBN-13: 978-0-8050-7557-1 / ISBN-10: 0-8050-7557-7
1. Turkey vulture—Juvenile literature. I. Jenkins, Steve, ill. II. Title.
QL696.C53S29 2007   598.9'2—dc22   2006030766

First Edition—2007 / Designed by Amelia May Anderson
The artist used cut-paper collage to create the illustrations for this book.
Printed in the United States of America on acid-free paper. ∞
10 9 8 7 6 5 4